12/07

FIRST BIOGRAPHIES

Tecumseh

Cassie Mayer

Heinemann Library
Chicago, Illinois

Customer Service **888-454-2279**

Visit our Web site at **www.heinemannlibrary.com**

Photo research by Tracy Cummins and Tracey Engel
Designed by Kimberly R. Miracle
Maps by Mapping Specialists, Ltd.
Printed and bound in China by South China Printing Company

10 09 08 07
10 9 8 7 6 5 4 3 2 1

10 Digit ISBN: 1-4034-9975-6 (hc)   1-4034-9984-5 (pb)

Library of Congress Cataloging-in-Publication Data
Mayer, Cassie.
  Tecumseh / Cassie Mayer.
    p. cm. -- (First biographies)
  Includes bibliographical references and index.
  ISBN-13: 978-1-4034-9975-2 (hc)
  ISBN-13: 978-1-4034-9984-4 (pb)
  1. Tecumseh, Shawnee Chief, 1768-1813--Juvenile literature. 2. Shawnee Indians--Kings and rulers--Biography--Juvenile literature. I. Title.
  E99.S35T1153 2008
  977.004'97317--dc22
  [B]
                        2007009987

Acknowledgements
The author and publisher are grateful to the following for permission to reproduce copyright material: ©Art Resource, NY **pp. 6** (Bildarchiv Preussicher Kulturbesitz), **10, 23b** (Bildarchiv Preussicher Kulturbesitz); ©The Bridgeman Art Library **p. 4** (American School, 19th century Peter Newark American Pictures, Private Collection); ©Corbis **pp. 5, 11** (Bettmann), **12** (Bettmann), **16** (Bettmann), **22** (Lee Snider/Photo Images); ©The Granger Collection **pp. 13, 17**; ©Library of Congress Prints and Photographs Division **pp. 14, 18, 19, 21, 23a**; ©North Wind Picture Archives **p. 20**; ©Ohio Historical Society **pp. 7, 8**; ©Publisher: Paramount Press Inc. **p. 15** (Robert Griffing).

Cover image reproduced with permission of ©The Bridgeman Art Library: American School, (19th century)/Peter Newark American Pictures, Private Collection. Back cover image reproduced with permission of ©The Granger Collection.

Every effort has been made to contact copyright holders of any material reproduces in this book.
Any omissions will be rectified in subsequent printings if notice is given to the publisher.

Contents

Introduction

Tecumseh was a great leader.
He was a Native American.

Native Americans were the first people
to live in America. They lived in tribes.

Tribes

A tribe is a group of people.
A tribe is like a family.

There were many tribes in North America.
Tecumseh was part of the Shawnee tribe.

Early Life

Tecumseh was born around 1768.

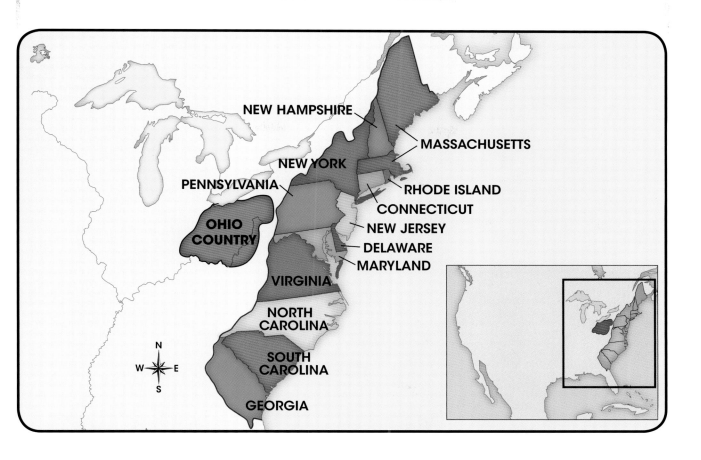

He lived in Ohio.

Other people lived in North America, too.

They moved there to start a new life.
They took land from Native Americans.

They wanted to own the land.
They wanted to build on the land.

Native Americans did not think anyone should own the land.

Tecumseh the Leader

When Tecumseh grew up, he became a great leader.

He led Native Americans to work together.
They worked together to save their land.

Tecumseh spoke with leaders of the United States.

He tried to get land back to
Native Americans.

War of 1812

The United States went to war with
Great Britain in 1812.

Tecumseh led Native Americans to fight in the war. They helped Great Britain fight the United States.

Tecumseh was a brave fighter.

Tecumseh was killed in a battle.

Why We Remember Him

Tecumseh was a great leader. He fought to save Native American land.

Picture Glossary

battle a fight that takes place during a war. Wars may have lots of battles.

tribe a group of people who live together

Timeline

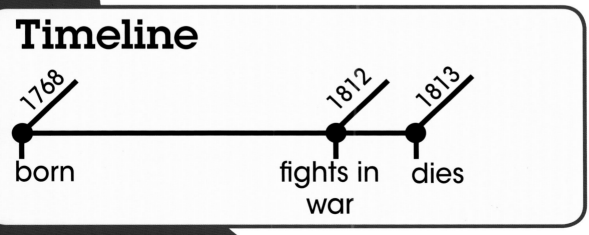

1768 — born

1812 — fights in war

1813 — dies

Index

Note to Parents and Teachers

This series introduces prominent historical figures, focusing on the significant events of each person's life and their impact on American society. Illustrations and primary sources are used to enhance students' understanding of the text.

The text has been carefully chosen with the advice of a literacy expert to enable beginning readers success while reading independently or with moderate support. An expert in the field of early childhood social studies curriculum was consulted to provide interesting and appropriate content.

You can support children's nonfiction literacy skills by helping students use the table of contents, headings, picture glossary, and index.